D1626421

THE LITTLE BOOK OF

GIN

TIPS

Juniper Berry

THE LITTLE BOOK OF

GIN

TIPS

Juniper Berry

A.

'When life hands you lemons,
make a gin and tonic.'

Anon.

1. There's no such thing as the 'perfect' gin and tonic. **General consensus is that a G&T should be either three parts tonic to one part gin, or two parts tonic to one part gin,** but it's all down to personal taste. Experiment and have fun finding the perfect G&T for you!

"General consensus is that a G&T should be either three parts tonic to one part gin, or two parts tonic to one part gin."

2. **Gin is simply flavoured vodka, and it couldn't be easier to make your own.** Add juniper berries to vodka in a clean, sterilised Kilner jar or bottle and leave for 24 hours. Add botanicals of your choice; popular botanicals include coriander seeds, cardamom pods, angelica seeds and lemon or orange peel. Leave for a further 24 hours, shaking occasionally. Sieve the botanicals and leave for another 24 hours. Run through a coffee filter or muslin cloth to filter out any sediment and your gin is ready to drink.

"Gin is simply flavoured vodka, and it couldn't be easier to make your own...

3. **Always have a stash of good-quality tonic water to hand.** Don't skimp on it; it's worth spending a bit of money as **it can totally transform your gin.** Always keep your tonic water in the fridge.

"Always have a stash of good-quality tonic water to hand ... it can totally transform your gin."

4. **Great gin pairings No. 1: grapefruit**
is a fantastic accompaniment to gin,
especially slightly sweeter infused
gins. Add a splash of grapefruit juice
to your G&T, or why not try a twist of
grapefruit in your Martini.

"Great gin pairings No. 1: grapefruit.

5. For a true taste of summer, **serve your gin and tonic with cucumber sandwiches for the perfect afternoon treat.**

"Serve your gin and tonic with cucumber sandwiches for the perfect afternoon treat. "

6. **There are many variations on the classic gin Martini, but the three constants are gin, vermouth and ice.** Martinis are always stirred and never shaken, and a good Martini should be stirred for around 30 seconds prior to straining. Shaking causes the ice to dilute the cocktail, which is then often cloudy and weak.

"There are many variations on the classic gin Martini, but the three constants are gin, vermouth and ice."

7. The choice of gins on the market can be overwhelming, but **ask your bartender for their recommendation;** it's a good place to start as they should be the experts.

"Ask your bartender for their recommendation.

8. **Store gin in a cool dark place, away from direct sunlight.** You can even store it in the fridge, or, for an ice-cold Martini, store your gin in the freezer (the alcohol content ensures it doesn't freeze). **If stored correctly, gin will last pretty much indefinitely.**

"Store gin in a cool dark place, away from direct sunlight. If stored correctly, gin will last pretty much indefinitely."

9. Always finish your gin and tonic before the ice melts, otherwise the ice will dilute the gin.

"Always finish your gin and tonic before the ice melts."

10.

Use gin to clean up your tarnished gold jewellery. Simply leave in gin overnight to work its magic.

"Use gin to clean up your tarnished gold jewellery."

11.

A 'twist' of lemon is exactly that.
Peel an inch or two of zesty lemon
skin, twist it over your Martini and
let the lovely lemony oil do its work.

"A 'twist' of lemon is exactly that.

12.

Bee's Knees: **a prohibition-era cocktail, it really is the bee's knees!** Add a splash of water to 2 teaspoons good-quality honey and mix until it dissolves. Combine 50ml gin (preferably bathtub gin!), 30ml fresh lemon juice and the honey with ice and shake. Strain and serve in a martini or coupe glass, garnish with a twist of lemon and edible flowers.

A prohibition-era cocktail, it really is the bee's knees...

13.

Join a gin club and/or attend gin tastings to sample lots of different types of gin without having to commit to the expense of full bottles.

"Join a gin club and/or attend gin tastings to sample lots of different types of gin."

14.

For a twist on a classic bake, try Kate's Gin Drizzle Loaf Cake. Weigh 4 eggs in their shells and weigh out the same amount of butter, caster sugar and flour. Whisk the eggs, butter and sugar together until fluffy and sieve in the flour and zest of 2 lemons. Pour the mixture into a lined loaf tin and bake for 35–45 minutes at 180°C until a skewer inserted comes out clean. Leave the cake to cool while you make the drizzle. Mix 6–8 shots of your favourite gin with the juice of 2 lemons and 130g granulated sugar. Prick the top of the cake with a fork and pour the drizzle over the top.

"For a twist on a classic bake, try Kate's Gin Drizzle Loaf Cake."

15.

The Tom Collins is so iconic they named a glass after it. **For a classic Tom Collins, mix 50ml gin, 25ml fresh lemon juice and 12.5ml sugar syrup in a tall glass with ice.** Top up with soda water. Garnish with a slice of lemon or orange and a maraschino cherry.

"For a classic Tom Collins, mix 50ml gin, 25ml fresh lemon juice and 12.5ml sugar syrup in a tall glass with ice."

16. For some grown-up cupcakes, bake a batch of regular vanilla or lemon cupcakes. Once cool, scoop out a small section on the top of each cupcake and fill with gin-infused lemon curd. **Add a dash of gin to your butter icing** and use to top the cupcakes. Garnish with lime zest.

Add a dash of gin to your butter icing.

17.

The Tom Collins tall glass gives a touch of classic elegance to a long gin drink.

"The Tom Collins tall glass gives a touch of classic elegance."

18.

An 'earthy' gin, such as Plymouth or Bath Gin, **is the perfect accompaniment to strong cheeses.**

"An 'earthy' gin is the perfect accompaniment to strong cheeses."

19. **Here's one for the coffee lovers – a turbo gin and tonic.** Fill a glass with ice. Make your gin and tonic to taste, leaving a little room at the top. Carefully pour in some fresh cold-brew coffee. Garnish with orange peel.

"Here's one for the coffee lovers –
a turbo gin and tonic...""

20.

Don't stir your gin and tonic too vigorously, as you'll risk losing the fizz.

"Don't stir your gin and tonic too vigorously.

21.

The French 75 (Soixante Quinze) **is a truly classic champagne cocktail.** Fill a cocktail shaker with ice and add 1 part gin, ½ part lemon juice and ½ part sugar syrup. Shake well and strain into a champagne flute. Top up with champagne and garnish with a twist of lemon.

"The French 75 is a truly classic champagne cocktail."

22.

For a more budget-friendly version of the French 75, **try an Italian 75.** Make in the same way, **and top with prosecco instead of champagne.**

"Try an Italian 75, and top with prosecco instead of champagne."

23.

Your favourite drink deserves to be served in a lovely glass. **Treat yourself to a special glass which will give you pleasure every time you use it.**

"Treat yourself to a special glass which will give you pleasure every time you use it. "

24.

Gin goes surprisingly well with meat, especially venison. **Try a sloe gin and blackberry sauce with roast venison, or** for fish lovers, **a creamy gin and lemon sauce is a perfect accompaniment for white fish.**

"Try a sloe gin and blackberry sauce with roast venison, or a creamy gin and lemon sauce is a perfect accompaniment for white fish. "

25.

Why not try substituting gin for vodka in your Bloody Mary.

"**Why not try substituting gin for vodka...**"

26.

The less vermouth in your Martini, the 'drier' it will be. For a classic Dry Martini use only a few drops of vermouth and stir with ice for 30 seconds then strain into a martini glass.

"The less vermouth in your Martini, the 'drier' it will be."

27.

Infuse your ice cubes to jazz up your gin and tonic. Try adding rosemary, cucumber or raspberries to your cubes. The possibilities are endless, and they look great in your glass.

"Infuse your ice cubes to jazz up your gin and tonic."

28.

Negroni is the perfect aperitif and couldn't be simpler to make. Add 1 part gin, 1 part Campari and 1 part red vermouth in a short glass, add ice and stir. Garnish with a twist of orange.

"Negroni is the perfect aperitif and couldn't be simpler to make."

29.

Use gin to remove those stubborn sticky labels or label residue; simply wipe with a gin-soaked cotton wool pad.

"Use gin to remove those stubborn sticky labels or label residue.

30.

For a long, refreshing drink, mix 1 part gin and 2 parts cranberry juice and top up with prosecco. Garnish with fresh cranberries.

"For a long, refreshing drink, mix 1 part gin and 2 parts cranberry juice and top up with prosecco."

31.

Gin and tonic ice lollies make a refreshing grown-up treat. Mix a batch of gin and tonic to taste with a good squeeze of fresh lemon or lime juice. Don't go too heavy on the gin otherwise it won't freeze. **Put fresh raspberries or slices of cucumber into ice lolly moulds, top up with your G&T mixture and freeze overnight.**

"Put fresh raspberries or slices of cucumber into ice lolly moulds, top up with your G&T mixture and freeze overnight."

32.

A beautiful bottle of gin is the perfect gift for that difficult to buy for person, and with so many to choose from, there's something to suit every taste, style and budget.

"A beautiful bottle of gin is the perfect gift for that difficult to buy for person."

33.

A Dirty Martini is flavoured with olive brine. Stir your gin, ice, vermouth and brine, strain into a glass, then add a whole or chopped olive to your Martini.

" " A Dirty Martini is flavoured with olive brine. " "

34.

An adults-only take on a childhood treat, try this gin and tonic float.
Make your gin and tonic to taste, pour into sundae glass and add a ball of lemon or lime sorbet. Garnish with basil leaves.

"An adults-only take on a childhood treat, try this gin and tonic float...

35.

For a refreshing gin, elderflower and prosecco cocktail, mix 1 part gin and a splash of elderflower cordial in a champagne flute, and top up with prosecco. Garnish with a sprig of lavender.

"For a refreshing gin, elderflower and prosecco cocktail..."

36. Always chill your martini glasses before use.

"Always chill your martini glasses before use."

37.

A slice of apple instead of the traditional lemon or lime **will transform your gin and tonic.** And the gin-soaked apple tastes utterly delicious.

"A slice of apple will transform your gin and tonic."

38. **Sloes are usually ripe for picking in October or November.** To make sloe gin, rinse and dry 500g sloes, then prick them all with a cocktail stick (messy, but essential). **Put the sloes in a large Kilner jar and add 1 litre gin and 250g caster sugar. Seal the jar and shake well**. Give the jar a good shake once a day for 10 days, then leave in a cool dark place for 2–3 months. Sieve the sloe gin through a muslin cloth and decant into bottles. Your sloe gin is ready to drink, but will mature over time.

"Sloes are usually ripe for picking in October or November. Put the sloes in a large Kilner jar and add 1 litre gin and 250g caster sugar. Seal the jar and shake well."

39. Before icing a cake that is covered with marzipan, **brush the surface of the marzipan with gin to prevent bacteria forming** between layers.

"Brush the surface of the marzipan with gin to prevent bacteria forming."

40.

Garnishes can totally transform your gin and tonic, and they look amazing. Why not try a sprig of rosemary, thyme, lavender or even some basil leaves. Or, for the fruit lovers, how about a skewer of mango and raspberries for a fruity hit.

"Garnishes can totally transform your gin and tonic, and they look amazing."

41.

The Southside Cocktail is a sophisticated gin-based take on a Mojito. Combine 50ml gin, 25ml fresh lime juice, 15ml sugar syrup and a handful of mint leaves in a cocktail shaker with ice. Shake, strain and serve in a martini glass, garnishing with extra mint leaves.

"The Southside Cocktail is a sophisticated gin-based take on a Mojito."

42.

**Great gin pairings No. 2: fiery
ginger beer** is a great mixer with gin.
Top with freshly grated ginger for
a real kick.

"Great gin pairings No. 2:
fiery ginger beer."

43. Rather than throw them away, **use leftover sloes from your sloe gin to make chocolate truffles.** Remove the stones from the sloes and heat 150ml double cream in a pan until almost boiling. Grate 150g dark chocolate and put in a bowl with 25g butter. Pour the heated cream over the chocolate and butter and stir until melted. Add the sloes and put the mix in the fridge to chill for an hour or two. Put a little cocoa powder in a shallow bowl and dust some on your hands. Roll a small spoonful of the truffle mix in your hands and roll in the cocoa powder.

Use leftover sloes from your sloe gin to make chocolate truffles.

44.

The *copa de balon* (or balloon glass) was traditionally used by Spanish gin drinkers. Eighty per cent of flavour is smell and the wide open balloon **makes the most of your gin's unique aromatics** and leaves room for fruit and/or sprigs of garnish. The stem stops the warmth of your hand melting the ice so your drink stays cold longer and is less diluted.

"The *copa de balon* makes the most of your gin's unique aromatics."

45.

For a refreshing and budget-friendly take on an Aperol Spritz, **simply add a splash of Aperol to your gin and tonic.** Serve with a wedge of orange.

"Simply add a splash of Aperol to your gin and tonic."

46.

Mulled gin is a perfect winter warmer. Simply combine 50ml sloe gin, 100ml apple juice and honey to taste. Add a cinnamon stick and cardamom pods and warm through on the hob. Serve immediately.

"Mulled gin is a perfect winter warmer.

47.

As Noël Coward famously said, '**A perfect Martini should be made by filling a glass with gin, then waving it in the general direction of Italy.**'

'A perfect Martini should be made by filling a glass with gin, then waving it in the general direction of Italy.'

48.

Believed to be drunk by sailors back in the day to prevent scurvy, a Gimlet is a very popular gin cocktail. **To make your own Gimlet, mix 50ml gin and 10ml lime cordial with ice. Strain into a martini glass and enjoy.**

"To make your own Gimlet, mix 50ml gin and 10ml lime cordial with ice. Strain into a martini glass and enjoy."

49.

Not for the faint-hearted, but gin can be used as an alternative to mouthwash. The alcohol kills bacteria. Just don't swallow!

" Not for the faint-hearted, but gin can be used as an alternative to mouthwash. "

50. Always drink your gin responsibly!

"**Always drink your gin** responsibly!"

For Tim – there's no better person with whom to drink gin. Janey and Jo, founder members of the French 75 Club. And everyone else I've enjoyed gin with – Sarah & Duncan, Sheila & John, Fraser & Kate, Tony & Penny, James & Deborah, Anthea & Paul, Vic & Pete, Franny & Steve, Maggie & Neil S, Maggie & Neil T, The Cronins, Holly & Mark, Sasha & Neil, Will & Cath, Cristina, Kate, Sam, Dusty, Laila, Suzy, Caroline and Annette, to name but a few.

Juniper Berry

> "Juniper Berry works in publishing. She spends most of her spare time searching for the perfect French 75 cocktail."

Little Books of Tips from
Absolute Press

Aga

Gardening

Allotment

Gin

Avocado

Golf

Beer

Herbs

Cake Decorating

Spice

Cheese

Tea

Coffee

Whisky

Fishing

Wine

If you enjoyed this book, try...

THE LITTLE BOOK OF

WHISKY

TIPS

"After sipping your whisky, wait for the finish.

"Old Fashioned is the name, but this whiskey cocktail has been in fashion for over a century.

ABSOLUTE PRESS

An imprint of Bloomsbury Publishing Plc

50 Bedford Square	1385 Broadway
London	New York
WC1B 3DP	NY 10018
UK	USA

www.bloomsbury.com

ABSOLUTE PRESS and the A. logo are trademarks of Bloomsbury Publishing Plc

First published in 2018

A catalogue record for this book is available from the British Library.
Library of Congress Cataloguing-in-Publication data has been applied for.

ISBN 13: 9781472956682

2 4 6 8 9 10 7 5 3

Printed and bound in China by Toppan Leefung Printing